NEW LIFE

Symbolic Meditations on the Birth of Christ Within

by Kathleen Wiley

Soulful Living, Inc.

D1227056

Copyright © 2015 by Kathleen Wiley
(pen name Adair Gillis)
All Rights Reserved.

No part of this book may be copied or reproduced
in any form without the express written consent of the author.
You can contact the author at
innerdivinespirit.blogspot.com or
adairgillis@gmail.com.

Cover Photo: Kathleen Wiley at Seabrook Island, South Carolina
Cover Design and Illustrations: DARLENE
Copyediting: Carol Wiley
Interior Design and Publishing Assistance: DARLENE

Most scripture passages from the New English Bible (NEB),
with occasional use of the Revised Standard Version of the Bible (RSV).

Softcover ISBN: 978-0-9915661-1-2
Digital ISBN: 978-0-9915661-0-5

1st Edition February 2014
2nd Edition November 2015

Published in the United States by:

Soulful Living, Inc.

DEDICATION

Dedicated to Mother Danae Ashley
for helping me birth the writings
of Inner Divine Spirit.

TABLE OF CONTENTS

INTRODUCTION

IVING IN conscious or knowing relationship to the Divine Spirit within us is the key to accessing and extending the beauty of our souls into our thinking, feeling, yearning, emoting, moving, acting, and creating. Reading, studying, and contemplating sacred texts, here The Holy Bible, stimulates our conscious connection to the Divine as the spiritual truths resonate with an innate inner knowing that is present because we are created in the image of God (Genesis 1).

Christians think of the Divine Within theologically as the Holy Spirit. Jews use the term Shekinah. Carl Jung used the term Self (with a capital S) to name the organizing principle of our psyche or soul and called it a part of God that God put in us so we know there is a God.

For me, Jung's model is the best bridge between psychology and spirituality. He recognized the presence of the Divine within us as inborn in the psychic structure he called the Self. In Jungian psychology, the Self is the psychic structure through which God manifests in our psyche/soul. The Self is the totality of our psyche/soul and the larger container of our conscious self or ego.

The ego is who we think we are, the sum total of our conscious experiences. The Self includes that plus all that is unknown in our personal self and the larger Mystery. Building a conscious relationship between the ego and the Self is primary in Jungian psychology. It is the ego-Self axis that gives us a felt sense of connection to the larger Mystery that we call God.

CULTIVATING CONSCIOUSNESS

CULTIVATING a conscious connection with the Self occurs as we experience the Holy Spirit or Divine in us. We experience God within through the stirrings of our life force in impulses, yearnings, automatic responses, sensations, and intuitions. Sometimes the seeds of the Self or Divine Within have grown into expressions that are destructive to us, yet the Divine is still present. Learning to relate to these expressions as symbolized in Bible stories and teachings provides a way to grow beyond the "natural man" to the "spiritual man." (Man refers to humanity as a whole, male and female.)

Natural humanity feels and believes itself to be at the mercy of outside forces (the environment, other people) and automatic responses. Spiritual humanity knows itself to be one with God and to have the ability to mediate the internal states of feelings and thoughts automatically triggered by outside events. Living in conscious relationship to our internal processes or sense of self/Self changes our internal experiences, changing our relationship to the outside world (other people, our work, and so forth).

MY JOURNEY AND WRITINGS

I GREW UP in the Baptist church practicing the discipline of daily meditations. I would read a scripture passage and explore it using various commentaries, Bible dictionaries, and other study materials. I struggled to understand the meaning theologically and practically for my life. My journey led me to academic degrees in Christian Education and Counseling. I was drawn to train professionally as a psychoanalyst in the tradition of Carl Jung because I see his work as the best marriage of psychology and spirituality.

I have been writing meditations on the scriptures with an eye towards what they mean about our psyche/soul. I consider the stories and images as symbols of our inner worlds, including our thoughts, feelings, sensations, intuitions, perceptions, impulses, and emotions. By contemplating the scriptures in this manner, we can access understanding of our selves as living beings who are manifestations of God. We begin to embrace and value who we are as everything in our nature holds a seed of the Divine.

The writings in this book are all related to the theme of new life. The seasons of Advent, Christmas, and Epiphany give us an opportunity to open to the new within our selves. The birth of the Christ symbolically happens every time we take an action or create a form that reflects the larger truth of who we are.

The symbolic Divine Child may emerge as a new attitude, behavior, change in habits, relationship, creative project, or feeling state. We know the energy is the Divine Within us because it changes us. We do something differently; we embody the energy in a new way of being with ourselves and with the outside world.

◆　◆　❖　◆　◆

I hope these writings will lead you to see the presence of the Divine emerging in your life now. Whether you agree or disagree with what I say, my hope is that the meditations will stimulate your heart to discern the voice of the Inner Divine Spirit that is accessible to those who seek it.

Kathleen Wiley

Note About Use of self/Self

IN JUNGIAN psychology, Self is the organizing principle of our psyche/soul and is the totality of our psyche. In contrast, the ego/self is an expression or extension of the Self. The ego/self is our conscious sense of self. It is what we think of as "I." Self, with a capital "S," is the larger whole of who we are. It holds all that is known and unknown in our nature. Jung once described Self as a part of God that God put in us so we know there is a God.

In this book, you will see use of both self and Self to refer to these different parts. Because of the way I use these terms, I also use the spelling our selves, rather than the standard ourselves.

CHAPTER I

DO NOT BE AFRAID
Luke 1:26–38

True safety lies with the Self/God Within. As we experience new desires, emotions, impulses, or longings, we may feel afraid. These messengers of our larger Self are like the angel Gabriel. They announce new life is coming. Do not be afraid!

Verses 29–31, "But she was deeply troubled by what he said and wondered what this might mean. Then the angel said to her, 'Do not be afraid, Mary, for God has been gracious to you.'"

The mistrust in our hearts
Blinds us to the gifts God has to offer
The gifts that come through Other
Other than me
Other than self
Other than that which I know
Other than that which I feign control over

How afraid we become
Our response to the unexpected Other
Sometimes an intrusion that hurts
Sometimes a wrong
Sometimes abuse

They color our expectations
The gifts get blocked by our defenses to Other

Defenses can save or kill
Wondering what is we look
With a discerning eye we seek to see what is
The primitive animal in me only knows survival
Fight or flight; Kill or be killed
The Divine spirit in me knows Being
Relating, Connecting, Joining
"Do not be afraid, Mary,
For God has been gracious to you."

We are called beyond our fear
To be open to the new
To the unexpected births
Beginnings that bring God's life to us
Embodying the essence of who we are
We nurture the life giving, life sustaining
We let go of the fear that blocks

Inner Reflection

Where do you feel troubled? What are the unexpected occurrences (feelings, phantasies, as well as outer world events) you are experiencing? What's changing that you had not anticpated? As you breathe, feel your connection to the Divine. Open to hear, see, and experience the gifts of God Within as you move with the new in your life.

CHAPTER 2

THE MYSTERY OF DARKNESS:
Job 23:1–9, 16–17

What we fear seeing in our selves almost always holds the key to greater living. We are restored to health and vitality in life as we willingly engage the unknown, the darkness and mystery of Self. The birth of the Christ child invites us to see beyond what we know and to willingly dialogue with parts of our nature that are problematic.

Verses 4, 15b, 17, "I would state my case before him and set out my arguments in full… when I think about him, I am afraid…yet I am not reduced to silence by the darkness nor by the mystery which hides him."

IN *"AN ANSWER TO JOB,"* Jung wrote about the psychological meaning of Job's suffering and its outcome. Jung's concluding premise was that God needed Job in order to see himself (God) more clearly. Job's attempts to stay in relationship to God, even when Job felt ignored, were finally met by God. Staying in relationship with God is what vindicated Job in the end.

Even though he was afraid, Job was bold enough to be willing to talk with God. As Job suffered, he struggled to understand what was happening and why. He reflected on his life, and he stated what he saw, believed, and experienced. He acknowledged the presence of the darkness and mystery of life, but he continued to speak from his experience and viewpoint.

Psychologically, Job's struggle with God symbolizes the ego's struggle with the Self (totality of psyche/soul, God Within). Ego is synonymous with the conscious self. Ego is formed by what we see and know about our selves. The darkness and mystery of the Self is all that is unconscious, including our reflexive personal patterns and automatic archetypal/instinctive templates.

Our suffering often originates from unconscious patterns that wreak havoc with our ego's emotions, feelings, perceiving, thinking, etc. We may feel "[the Self's] hand is heavy on me in my trouble." At these times, the ego may try to go it alone. We may resort to known patterns of behaviors and relationships with others and our selves even if the patterns are problematic and limiting. The ego's reliance only on what is known, without openness to seeing the unconscious Self, is ultimately self-defeating. It is in the willingness to engage the unknown, the darkness and mystery of the Self, that we are restored to health and vitality in life.

Inner Reflection

Take a few minutes to acknowledge where you are suffering in any way—physically, emotionally, mentally, spiritually. Look to see what you know about the situation and yourself. Pay attention to the emotions and affects (pervasive moods or overshadowing feelings) that are present and note what they trigger in your body and mind. State what you know to yourself and the Self.

In this way, build a relationship between yourself and what is present. Open to see the workings of the darkness and mystery of the Inner Divine Spirit that can bring healing/wholeness.

CHAPTER 3

GOD COMES WITH FIRE:
Psalm 50:3

Mary and Joseph journeyed a long way immediately before the birth of Jesus. We can only imagine the difficulties and turmoil they experienced. Often, the birth of something new in our life, inner and outer, is preceded by a shake up. The peace and calm we desire comes after we make room for the new aspect of our larger Self/God Within.

Verse 3, "Our God comes and will not be silent;
a fire devours before him, and around
him a tempest rages."

YEARS AGO, I read an author who stated that every time we encounter God it is a crisis event. The psalmist seems to affirm this view. He paints God's emerging presence in our lives as a raging storm and a consuming fire. The peace and calm we desire usually comes secondary to the shake up and turmoil we feel when the Divine Presence makes itself known.

We all have times when we want something to be different in our lives. We are not happy, we feel restless, we long for our heart's desires, we feel an urge to move and grow. Yet, we stay stuck. We go unconscious—we numb out, we deny reality, we pretend. In these moments, it sometimes takes a whirlwind, thunderstorm, or fire to wake us up.

The whirlwind, thunderstorm, or fire may show up in our inner world first, and then extend to the outer world of home, work, relationships, etc. It may also begin with an unexpected event in the outer world that brings distress and upset. Our body sensations, feelings, thoughts, and intuitions may whirl around uncontrollably. We may feel consumed/obsessed with an idea or a memory or a struggle. We may feel caught by an energy that we do not understand or know how to relate to. In these moments, God Within/the Self is demanding our attention and action.

We chose, consciously or by default, how we respond to the Self's demand for our attention. We can feel punished by the Divine Essence and act like a victim. We can hold on to the old sense of self and way of living, and resist moving forward.

Or, we can welcome the workings of God Within/the Self and look in the turmoil to see where and how the Divine is speaking. We can consciously go with the transformative fire/spirit and let go of the false self attitudes, behaviors, relationships, etc. to which we hold.

As we begin to identify with the Inner Divine Self, we have courage to withstand the storms and fires of change. Death and destruction always precedes birth and creation. Old ways and structures must go for the new to emerge. Our souls are always seeking to live more fully and beautifully through our egos and in our lives. Nothing in natures stands still; we are either growing or dying. The Inner Divine Spirit propels us towards greater Self-expression with "raging tempests" and "fire" when necessary. △

Inner Reflection

Take a few minutes to reflect on where you feel the Divine's emerging presence in your life. What are the "tempests" and "fires" you are experiencing? Ask the Inner Divine Spirit to help you see and know the seeds of your Divine Self in these experiences. Welcome the destruction of all the attitudes, emotions, and behaviors that are not true to your Divine Essence. Have courage to stand in the truth of who you really are.

CHAPTER 4

LETTING GO OF FORM:
Exodus 32:21–34

Life starts from the Mystery of the Limitless Light, "the world without form and void." The birth of a baby always brings a world that is constantly changing. The old order is upset. It has to change. Our willingness to let go of the forms of how we used to be, what we used to do, etc. is necessary to grow the new life that comes.

Verses 22-23, "Aaron replied, 'Do not be angry sir, the people were deeply troubled; that you well know. And they said to me, 'Make us gods to go ahead of us, as for this fellow Moses, who brought us up from Egypt, we do not know what has become of him.'"

HOW OFTEN our impatience and unknowing is the cause of our difficulties! Like the Israelites in today's scripture, we get antsy not knowing something, so we set about making what is known into gods. We cling to ideas, beliefs, values, or perceptions with which we are comfortable instead of seeking the felt presence of the Divine. We forget that life starts from the Mystery of the Limitless Light, "the world without form and void." We do not like the void or the darkness, so we create ways of living that thwart our libido/ life force. We may even lose sight of our heart's desires (which flow from the Inner Divine Spirit) as our libido/life force is captured in something stagnant.

Wherever we are attached to form, we eventually become stuck, lifeless, or empty. The form may be a relationship, a job situation, a habit, a belief, a thought pattern, etc. Forms are a necessary part of the human experience as we are called to embody—to manifest. Forms are problematic only when they become more important than the Spirit. When we hold to ways of living that thwart the flow of the Inner Divine Spirit, we make those forms gods.

The Israelites had practice living in relationship to a fixed, tangible god of the golden calf. When troubled, they were unwilling to stay in the fluid, ever-evolving relationship with the Divine Spirit. When we are troubled, we tend to reach for what we know. Like the wandering Israelites, we return to what was known in the past. Our allegiances go to the relationships (to people, places, structures, teachings, beliefs, feelings, desires, and thoughts) that have been in place, instead of opening to the Spirit in the unknown or changing.

Inner Reflection

I invite you to consider where you are loyal to the gods that are man-made. What are the beliefs, relationships, feeling states, habit patterns, etc. that you know thwart your Inner Divine Spirit? Where do you feel lifeless, stuck, or as if you are dying? Where are you afraid of change?

Open to feel what, where, and towards whom the Inner Divine is moving you (in the inner and outer worlds). Be courageous and stay with the discomfort until you sense in your body and mind the presence of the Divine flow. Set sacred intention to follow the energy of the Self/God Within.

CHAPTER 5

SEEKING GOD'S SUPPORT THROUGH THE SELF/GOD WITHIN:
Galatians 1:1–18

When we act in obeisance to the prevailing outer world standards, we often persecute parts of our selves that are expressions of the Self/God Within. Our learned attitudes and beliefs may be threatened; we respond to the new with the violence of self-degradation, self-hatred, etc. Like Mary and Joseph and the wise men, we must chose to receive and act on the protective direction of the Self/God Within. Paul did this in response to his life-changing encounter with God.

Verse 10, "Does my language now sound as if I were canvassing for men's support? Whose support do I want but God's alone? Do you think I am currying favor with men? If I still sought men's favor, I should be no servant of Christ."

HOW WE want to fit in! Our need to belong, to feel acceptance, and to feel loved is a prime motivator of our behavior. We start deferring to other people before we have the cognitive abilities and conscious awareness to be aware of our inner guidance. This happens automatically as an infant/child is dependent on the caregivers, usually parents and siblings.

Our birth family is the first group to which we belong. So much of how we express and think about our selves is rooted in the early life experiences that take place in our family.

The realm of influence extends beyond family to society as the institutions of church, school, media, etc. shape our mores.

We know the story of Paul, known as Saul when he persecuted Christians. Steeped in the tradition of his family, church, and the prevailing beliefs of his day, Paul lived a life that was counter to following the Inner Divine Spirit. He had a numinous experience and was completely transformed. He states in the scripture above that his actions (language) are now prompted by the guidance of Christ. Psychologically, we encounter Christ through the Self, the totality of psyche that Jung described as a part of God that God put in us so we know there is a God.

We can think of Paul as symbolic of an aspect of our selves. When we act in obeisance to the prevailing outer world standards, we often persecute other parts of our selves that are expressions of the Self/God Within. This energy comes up in self-deprecating comments, self-demeaning attitudes, hostile criticism, deadening beliefs, etc. We reflexively shoot down new ideas, yearnings, impulses, creative fantasies, emotions, and feelings. We direct an underlying feeling of murderous self-hatred towards aliveness that does not fit within the cultural (or familial) milieu.

The first part of individuation, living the truth of our soul, requires discernment between the truth of who we are as a soul and who we have learned to be. Affirming the ways in which we live that are aligned expressions of our soul lets us see those ways that are not our truth. Hopefully, there is overlap where our authentic Self is expressed in ways we have learned. We know the places this Self-expression is not happening because we feel a dis-ease with our self.

In the places of dis-ease, we have an opportunity to seek a greater, clearer, more conscious connection to the Self/God Within. We seek this connection through our self-reflection; dialogue with the inner states of desires, feelings, thoughts, etc.; paying attention to our dreams for instruction; spiritual disciplines of meditation, journaling, prayer; listening with the ears of our hearts, not just our rational minds; asking the Inner Divine for transformation; and being open to the movements of the Inner Divine even when we are caught off guard (as was Saul)!

Inner Reflection

Take a few minutes to reflect on your current inner state of being. Where has the Saul energy of persecution been active? Where have you moved to acceptance and nurturing of your true self? How are your acceptance and nurture manifesting in your self-talk, actions, and relationships? Where do you get caught by the adaptive/false self that seeks to please others? Set sacred intention to follow the energies of the Self/God Within by acting from your heart.

CHAPTER 6

CYCLING—OPPOSITES OF CREATION AND DESTRUCTION:

Ecclesiastes 3:1–15

"He has made everything in its season." There is a time for birthing and a time for dying. We need to know how to align with the cycles of creation and destruction, to discern what is needed when. The larger Self/God Within guides us to know when we are willing to act on the guidance. Mary and Joseph acted on God's guidance even when it was inconvenient and socially awkward. They destroyed old conventions to give birth to the Christ.

Verse 11, "He has made everything to suit its time; moreover, he has given men a sense of time past and future, but no comprehension of God's work from beginning to end."

TODAY'S scripture is a familiar passage that is often quoted flippantly during upheaval or change. We tend to overlook the powerful spiritual truth that everything exists with its opposite; everything cycles from creative to destructive. We see this principle at work in nature in the seasons. Spring brings new growth—beautiful flowers and leaves. Summer hosts the fullness of the new life. In the fall, flowers and leaves die; the (seemingly) barrenness of winter then comes. We do not question why it is this way. We accept it as a given, and we live within the cycles and do what is appropriate for that time.

The cycles of creation and destruction, as seen in the seasons of nature, are at work within our bodymind. Consider the processes of metabolism, with the tearing down of tissues (catabolism) and the building up of tissues (anabolism). Psychic (or soul) energies within us exist as pairs of opposites. They are bipolar; they have a light, creative, expansive side and a dark, destructive, constrictive side.

Reading the referenced passage gives us several examples of these opposites: birthing and dying, planting and uprooting, killing and healing, pulling down and building up, weeping and laughing, mourning and dancing, scattering and gathering, embracing and refraining, seeking and losing, keeping and throwing away, tearing and mending, being silent and speaking, loving and hating, warring and keeping peace.

Our culture and institutions have demonized the dark and destructive forces; anything that is not light and sustaining has been labeled as wrong or an illness. Such an attitude prevents us from effectively living within the seasons of our own (psychic) nature. Instead of aligning with our energy cycles, we move with learned attitudes and beliefs, asserting our ego while ignoring the inner knowing of the Self/God Within.

When we begin new projects or relationships where we lack desire and energy, it is like planting new seeds in the winter instead of the spring. When we hold on to the forms (relationships, jobs, interests, ways of experiencing, attitudes about our selves, habit patterns) that are dying and destructive to us, we miss the work of fall which includes raking up the old, dying leaves and clearing the ground for new growth. Often the suffering we experience is created by our ego's choices to hold onto learned expectations and values instead of aligning with the seasons of psyche/soul and the heart. We forget or deny the truth "for everything its season."

Inner Reflection

Take a few minutes to review the opposites listed from the scripture passage. Ask the Inner Divine Spirit to show you where these energies are at work in you. Consider all four planes—physical (health, eating, exercise, environment), emotional (feelings, relationships, needs, wants, automatic response patterns), mental (relationships to self and others, beliefs, values), and spiritual (openness to the Mystery and the Inner Divine Spirit). Be courageous and begin to live according to the cycles of your own psyche/soul.

CHAPTER 7

BEING EXPOSED
Hebrews 4:11–16

When we encounter the Divine, we are seen. When we are seen, we are exposed. Nothing is hidden. We see truths about our selves that we have avoided. We have to search our selves to hold all the truths of our nature together. We can imagine that Mary and Joseph had to search their hearts multiple times as they lived the life-changing events of the birth of the Christ child. They had to choose to follow the Mystery. We, too, must search our hearts and chose to go with the birth of the Self/God Within as new aspects of our selves show up.

Verse 13, "There is nothing in creation that can hide
from him; everything lies naked and exposed to the eyes
of the One with whom we have to reckon."

Being naked with our self
What a complicated thing
Or what a simple thing
Conscious knowing of our fullness

We dismiss what we know
Fear of being wrong, not enough
Defenses, denials, guilt, shame
Scatter bits of our self

We wonder why we feel empty
Confused, disoriented, unfocused
Hiding from our self
We lose access to our true nature

Fullness means wholeness
Light and dark, helpful and hurtful
Mundane and holy
All expressions of the Self

Our true Self knows what's in us
Ready to offer guidance
Will we hide? Or stand naked?
With our full truth we are whole

THE ESOTERIC spiritual tradition has a beautiful image of a naked man looking towards a naked woman with outstretched arms ready to receive. She has her arms raised above her and is looking to receive from the Archangel Raphael. The Archangel, a symbol of the Self/God Within, has outstretched arms positioned as if giving to the woman and man. There is nothing hidden between the man and the woman. All is exposed.

The image calls us to know the desired relationship between the aspects of Self. Our conscious ego (the man) looks to our subconscious self (the woman) who looks to the Divine Self (Archangel) for guidance. It is a relationship where we, with our ego consciousness, realize that our truest guidance and prompting comes from the Divine Self through our subconscious. We often refer to this subconscious channel as the heart. Looking in our heart, versus our head, we find the Divine guidance we need.

Clearing the channel of communication between the levels of consciousness demands that our ego/conscious sense of self realize that it is not in charge. There is the known self, and there is the Self, the totality of psyche that is always bigger than our known self. Psychologically, the Self is "the One with whom we have to reckon."

We encounter the larger Self every day in our felt senses. Desired and undesired, bidden and unbidden encounters present us unknown pieces of self/Self that are always present. Our emotions, sensations, impulses, desires, fantasies, and thoughts hold a seed of the Self. As we cultivate a relationship between our ego, subconscious, and transcendent Self, we begin to differentiate the Divine's guidance from the 'should,' 'must,' and 'ought to' thoughts that we internalized from outside authorities (parents, church, school, society).

Our psyche is a whole. It is a totality of all the energies of the Divine that express psychologically in the instincts of hunger, sexuality, aggression, self-reflection, and creativity. We build conscious access to these energies by tending the experiences of life. When we pay attention to our impulses and our felt sense (what our senses are experiencing), we meet the Divine energy that is our life force. We feel the sensations and emotions that evoke related images, impulses, beliefs, and ideas. We courageously face and stand in relationship to what shows up inside us. In this way, a life-giving reckoning occurs as our sense of self is strengthened and expanded by integrating the previously unknown bits of Self that constantly make themselves known through our instinctive responses.

Inner Reflection

In your mind's eye, visualize the image described in the first paragraph. Set sacred intention to be naked to yourself, to no longer hide from your self/Self. Welcome whatever emotions, feelings, thoughts, sensations, and intuitions you have pushed away. Be courageous and seek to know the seed of your self that is showing up in the desired or undesired state.

CHAPTER 8

A REVELRY FOR NEW LIFE
Luke 2:6–7

Nature has its own timing in the birthing process! When it's time to deliver, it's time. When something in our nature is ready to be born, we feel an energetic pressure for it to happen. We can choose to tend the new life, or we can ignore it and let it die. Mary tended the birth. She cared for the Christ child. Let us tend the Divine being born in us.

Verses 6-7, "While they were there, the time came for her to deliver her child. And she gave birth to her firstborn son and wrapped him in strips of cloth and laid him in a manger, because there was no place for them in the inn."

Wren slept on my door
Reminding me of resourcefulness, adaptability
The Virgin Mary adapted
A Divine seed began to grow
An unexpected birth changed her forever

Will I tend the new?
The creative that cries for holding, feeding, cleaning up
A new born part of me needing care
Sleep deprived, as Mary must have been
How will I do it all?

Wren shows me the way
Nesting in unusual, creative ways; focused
Purity of heart driving
She nestled in the corner
As if hidden—protected from the elements

Our creative babies need protection
From the heat of our criticism
The drowning of our insecurity
The flitting of our mind's focus
And the inertia of inaction

The door we need is the
Portal to Self, The Divine threshold,
where we meet God
Spirit becomes matter
Ego and soul are one
We know our larger truth

Mary lived her truth
It wasn't what she expected
She changed her course, Joseph too
Convenience didn't matter
A simple manger did it

Wren calls me to use what's here
To be held in the place I Am,
to hold the gifts that come
Receiving the Divine seeds
Creating with what's before me
Moving with life as it grows

Inner Reflection

Where are you birthing something new? What is growing
unexpectedly in your life? Desires? Habits? Attitudes? Creative
Projects? Responsibilities? What are the resources available to
you as you live into the new? Look to see what is being offered
to support you. Set sacred intention to move with the birth of
the Divine in your life today.

CHAPTER 9

HAVING NO ANXIETY:
Philippians 4:4–7

The Christmas story is filled with examples of the close presence of the Divine. We can only imagine the anxiety Mary and Joseph, the Wise Men, and the shepherds must have felt as they received the birth of the Christ. They followed the promptings of Divine Messengers and had the protection and shelter needed to honor the new. We are guided every day through the intelligences in our body and mind. We must remember the Divine is near.

Verse 6, "The Lord is near; have no anxiety, but in everything make your requests known to God in prayer and petition with thanksgiving. Then the peace of God, which is beyond our utmost understanding, will keep guard over your hearts and your thoughts, in Christ Jesus."

ANXIETY is a common human experience. We all know what it feels like because we have experienced it in some form. The first definition of anxiety in Webster's Dictionary is "painful or apprehensive uneasiness of mind usually over an impending or anticipated ill." The Advent season ushers in a time of anxiety for most as we attend to the outer demands of the season's celebrations. We get caught feeling as if we have to do it all ourselves, or something bad will happen. The anxiety sets in!

When we shift our focus to the symbolic, spiritual meaning of the Advent and Christmas seasons, we are offered an image of the way out of the anxiety—preparing for the birth of the Divine Child within us. Symbolically, the birth of Christ reminds us of the presence of the Divine Within/the Self (versus the ego/self) that is ever seeking ways to manifest in us. Our body experiences, our emotions, feelings, thoughts, and actions are the "children" of our psyche/soul. They are shaped according to the beliefs and resulting affects, both those that are conscious or known to our ego and those that are unconscious or unknown to our conscious sense of self, with which the ego/self is most identified.

The affirmation "The Lord is near" reminds us that the energy of the Christ, the Divine Essence Within, is close to us. We do not have to travel anywhere to know God; we only have to look within and be willing to see and hear the truth of our psyche/soul.

When we turn our attention inward, we begin to consciously connect to the energies of the Self by dialoguing with whatever is there. The inner dialogue, known as active imagination, goes on all the time without conscious attention. Think about the conflicting voices in your head: "I want a brownie… No, you do not. You need to lose weight." "He's bad for me. I can't see him…I can't leave him alone." "I want something to be different…I can't do anything different."

By attending to our inner dialogue and consciously engaging whatever "voices" or feelings we have, we open to understanding ourselves more fully. We can then build a relationship to whatever energies are behind the thoughts, feelings, emotions, etc. that we are experiencing. This relationship facilitates and invites an inner shift from anxious, problematic states to peaceful, joyous ones. In this way, "prayer and petition with thanksgiving" can be made to God as we live in relationship to the Self.

Inner Reflection

Take a few minutes to shift your focus to your inner process and to call on the Inner Divine Spirit for guidance. Acknowledge your anxieties and see where they live in your body. Dialogue with the Divine Within and ask for clarity and direction regarding these anxieties. Open to the birth of new ways of being—perceiving, feeling, thinking, and moving—that will move you toward peace and joy.

CHAPTER 10

BEING MADE NEW:
Ephesians 4:17–32

Christmas offers an opportunity to seek the birth of the new in our lives. Our call, the call from the Self/God Within, is to be "made new in mind and spirit."

Verse 24, "You must be made new in mind and spirit, and put on the new nature of God's creating, which shows itself in the just and devout life called for by the truth."

Colossians 3:3, "I repeat, you died; and now your life lies hidden with Christ in God."

"I REPEAT, you died! What a wonderful reminder to keep moving forward, to not circle back to the past, to not pick up what we have left behind! Our call, the call from the Self/God Within, is to be "made new in mind and spirit." We may know what is problematic for us but not know how to do anything differently. A new state of consciousness is required for new options.

Jung stated that a problem cannot be resolved in the state of consciousness in which it was conceived. We must get "above it" or "below it"—see and experience it in a different way. To do this, we must acknowledge, own, and relate to the state of consciousness we are in.

Seeing what is, where we are, and how we are is the first step in transformation. Knowing the lay of our inner landscape (thoughts, feelings, sensations, intuitions, emotions, perceptions) allows us to navigate towards new life. Too often, we repeat history instead of living the present moment. Our energies are stuck; we respond to the present person, situation, impulse, etc. as if we were in a past relationship. Fears pull us backwards even though we have a taste for something new. When we remember to reach for the larger Self, the connection to God Within us, we can differentiate the past from the present. We can see the life that "lies hidden with Christ in God." We experience openings to a new mind and spirit.

Change in action requires a change in mind and spirit. How we think, the energies we cultivate with our words (spoken and unspoken), the images we hold, and the fantasies we play out create our experiences. If we want different experiences, a different life, we have to create and hold passionate images of what we want. We have to fuel the fire of desire to create an embodied state that energizes us towards the new. Moments of clinging to the past, replaying failures, nursing disappointments, tolerating self deprecation, or dismissing our resources (inner and outer) have to be left behind. Clinging to the Self, God Within, is what is needed.

Our egos, the conscious sense of self, have only a limited awareness of the reality of who we are. The Self, the totality of psyche, holds the big picture. Consciously seeking a connection to the Self facilitates new life; we begin to sense the possibilities of our souls. A conscious relationship between our egos and our Selves changes the way we see things. It moves us from the tunnel vision of who we think we are to the bigger reality of who we are on a soul level. The shift from identifying with our little selves (egos) to knowing our selves as a child of God opens us to new life.

Inner Reflection

Be courageous! Cultivate a stronger relationship to the Self by listening for the still, small voice of God that speaks in the word-less knowing of your bodymind. Pay attention to your intuitions, your inner teacher. Use your intellect to discern the differences between now and the past. Act with the promptings of the Inner Divine Spirit. Remind yourself as often as needed, "the old me has died, the new me lies with the Self/God Within."

CHAPTER 11

ONE BODY:

1 Corinthians 12:27–13:3

The Christmas story is a beautiful reminder of our interconnectedness and how we all matter. Mary and Joseph needed one another to bring the Christ child into the world. The wise men and shepherds were affected; they went to greet and honor the baby Jesus. We affect one another positively as we give birth to the Divine in our nature.

Verse 27, "Now you are Christ's body, and each of you a limb or organ of it."

PAUL'S statement to the Christian community at Corinth, "Now you are Christ's body, and each of you a limb or organ of it," gives a picture of how we, humanity, are interrelated and "one." Each of us has a place, role, and function in the collective. The collective is a whole in which we affect each other constantly, as we are connected energetically because we share "Christ's Body."

"Christ's Body" can be understood as a symbol for the collective unconscious. Jung postulated the presence of the collective unconscious within the human psyche as the source of universal templates (patterns of experiencing and behaving) that we have in common because we are born human. He observed the interconnectedness of humanity as he tracked the appearance of mythological and religious stories and symbols. The same themes and images appeared worldwide, simultaneously, without exchange between cultures.

For Jung, the simultaneous appearance of the templates (known as archetypes) proved a shared source of consciousness. It also suggests that what comes to be known in one person stimulates or parallels that knowing in another. The collective unconscious, or "Christ's body," is the vehicle through which this happens.

We may feel disconnected from other people and as if no one would notice our absence. Sometimes, we feel as if we do not matter. Yet, we all feel the effects when an organ or limb of our physical body is not "present"—not functioning. It does matter!

In the same way, we each matter; the whole of humanity needs our presence and functioning. A healthy body needs all parts fulfilling their raison d'être. So it is with the collective and us. We need each other to live as who we are created to be. Our individual and collective health is dependent on knowing our essence and living accordingly. We experience openings to a new mind and spirit.

Change in action requires a change in mind and spirit. How we think, the energies we cultivate with our words (spoken and unspoken), the images we hold, and the fantasies we play out create our experiences. If we want different experiences, a different life, we have to create and hold passionate images of what we want. We have to fuel the fire of desire to create an embodied state that energizes us towards the new. Moments of clinging to the past, replaying failures, nursing disappointments, tolerating self deprecation, or dismissing our resources (inner and outer) have to be left behind. Clinging to the Self, God Within, is what is needed.

Our egos, the conscious sense of self, have only a limited

awareness of the reality of who we are. The Self, the totality of psyche, holds the big picture. Consciously seeking a connection to the Self facilitates new life; we begin to sense the possibilities of our souls. A conscious relationship between our egos and our Selves changes the way we see things. It moves us from the tunnel vision of who we think we are to the bigger reality of who we are on a soul level. The shift from identifying with our little selves (egos) to knowing our selves as a child of God opens us to new life.

Inner Reflection

Take a few minutes to reflect on your sense of self. What do you know about yourself? What is a mystery? What do you believe about who you are and who you are to become? Where are you living as who you truly are? Where are you caught in a false persona/role? Ask the Self/God Within to help you see more clearly and fully the totality of who you are and your raison d'être. Be courageous, and act on what you receive.

CHAPTER 12

KEEP YOUR HOUSE IN ORDER:
Isaiah 65:17–25

During the holiday season, we need to be reminded to tend to our selves. We can get separated from our selves by giving too much. We give in to outer world demands and unrealistic self-expectations. Follow Mary and Joseph's example to tend to what you need.

Verses 21–22, "Men shall build houses and live to inhabit them, plant vineyards and eat their fruit; they shall not build for others to inhabit nor plant for others to eat."

WHAT AN interesting injunction to the Israelites as the prophet Isaiah describes the New Jerusalem, symbolic of the new world! So much of mainstream religious belief supports doing for others even if detrimental to us! No doubt, there is a need for charity within community in the world and within our selves. Perhaps, the scripture is speaking symbolically, noting the reality that each of us is to build and inhabit the house of our bodymind and personality and to plant the seeds of nourishment we need for our selves.

Too often, we try and grow within our personality and bodymind what others plant for us— their ideas and opinions of who we should be. Or, we get caught trying to make other people what or whom we think they should be. Our energy is spent trying to "fix" or "save" others from their choices. We forget that the Divine lives within each of us and is constantly manifesting in our bodyminds and personalities. Our experience is conditioned from the moment of conception by outside factors, thus our body, mind, and personality reflect both the influence of the Divine Within/Self and the outer environment (which includes relationships).

The flow of the Divine Spirit into our bodymind is described in the Kabbalah on The Tree of Life, which is an image of the spiritual energies within us. The Tree shows ten spheres that represent emanations or essences of God as they flow into the soul of the world and the soul of humanity.

The Tree is divided into three triangles: The highest triad is known as The Supernal Triangle. It includes three spheres: Limitless Light, Wisdom, and Understanding. These are the energies of the Divine in their purest, numinous state. As the pure moves toward embodiment, it flows into the three spheres of Mercy and Compassion, Strength and Severity, Beauty and Balance; they compose the second triangle.

This second Triangle of the Higher Self is the expression of God Within our psyche/soul. (In analytical psychology, the use of Self with a capital S denotes this triangle). These energies carry and extend the essences of the Supernal Triangle so they are accessible to us in our bodies and minds. These energies flow and extend into the third triangle of the personality, which includes the three spheres of Victory (of our Heart's Desires), Glory (of our Intellect), and the Foundation (of our vital soul or animal/reflexive consciousness). Everything we sense, feel, think, or intuit has a seed of the Divine in it!

The final sphere on the Tree, in the triangle of the personality, is the Kingdom of Earth and our bodymind. This sphere is known as the Bride because it is our embodied self that the

Higher Self, or Christ Within, seeks to be its mate. The spiritual promptings we experience are an instinctive drive for our ego to develop awareness and seek union with the Inner Divine Spirit.

Growth from conception to adulthood requires adapting to the outer environment and its demands. For this reason, the ego often becomes wed to adapted and adopted ways of experiencing, being, and doing. Instead of perceiving and moving and living as prompted from God Within, we are driven by the old, learned order. The work of individuation and incarnation involves shifting from living as taught by others to living as led by the Inner Divine Spirit. When we make this shift, we build "our house" and "plant our vineyards."

Inner Reflection

What is the state of your "house" and "vineyards"? Consider what is happening in your bodymind physically, emotionally, mentally, and spiritually. You may reflect on the named energies of The Tree of Life and see what comes to mind around each. Let your Inner Divine Spirit guide you to see how your reflexive responses, thoughts, intellectual processes, passions and desires hold seeds of God Within. As you see the seeds of the Self/God Within, open to their growth in the form that best reflects and holds the purity of the Divine in you.

CHAPTER 13

THE UNION OF OPPOSITES:
Psalm 119:89–96

The birth of the Christ brings reconciliation. Within our psyches/souls, something is united every time a bit of the larger Self/God Within is born. We consciously invite the Divine by holding opposing energies in dialogue until the union occurs.

Verse 96, "I see that all things come to an end, but thy commandment has no limit."

Ephesians 2: 13–22, Verses 14, 16, "For he is himself our peace, Gentiles and Jews, he has made the two one, and in his own body of flesh and blood has broken down the enmity which stood like a dividing wall between them…This was his purpose, to reconcile the two in a single body to God through the cross, on which he killed the enmity."

WHEN WE consider the scripture stated from a viewpoint of analytical psychology, each of the characters is an aspect of our psyche/soul. The Gentiles and the Jews can be seen as symbols of the instincts and archetypes within us.

Instincts are automatic, reflexive impulses to respond to stimuli in certain ways; archetypes are automatic, unbidden affective (feeling) states that create desire that propels us to move in certain ways. Instincts are like the infrared end of the light spectrum; archetypes are like the ultraviolet. Instincts are associated with the body and release somatic tension; archetypes are associated with the spirit and bring new expressions of our self. We all have suffered from the split between the two, as the Gentiles and the Jews suffered from their division.

As Christ made the two one, referring to the Gentiles and Jews, God Within us unites antagonistic aspects of our natures. The antagonistic aspects usually show up as an impulse to respond in a certain way (for example, eat for comfort, purchase something that catches the eye, call an "ex" who is hurtful to you because you feel lonely, end a relationship, or change jobs) and a desire for something different (eating only when physically hungry, avoiding shopping on impulse, keeping healthy boundaries and finding new friends, or wanting the relationship or job). We experience

opposition within our selves in innumerable ways that foster ill will or hatred of our self.

We have all felt volleyed back and forth between opposites in our nature. We decide on one way, but the other way creeps up and interferes. The ego alone does not have the capacity to resolve the conflict in a way that unites the opposites and creates a unifying third (option). The Self, or God Within us, does have that capacity, just as Christ had that effect with the Gentiles and Jews.

In analytical psychology, Jung wrote about the phenomenon of the Transcendent Function. Simply stated, the Transcendent Function is an organic process that kicks in when we consciously relate to opposing positions and hold both within our bodymind simultaneously. When we consciously hold opposing positions, the uniting third position emerges spontaneously. Our tendency is to align with one side and dismiss the other. Thus, we continue being tossed to and fro within our selves. To invite the Transcendent Function, we must consciously experience and hold the antagonistic energies together until the third emerges.

The cross is an apt symbol for the expression of God Within through the Transcendent Function. The opposites (literally, vertical and horizontal arms that we could say symbolize archetype and instinct) are united. A sacrifice is made as each must yield to the other to form a union.

Inner Reflection

Take a few minutes to acknowledge the conflicts within you. Flesh out the opposites by feeling into them. What are the ideas, beliefs, body sensations, emotions, and images that accompany them? (Journaling can be helpful in doing this.) Hold the opposites together and open for the Inner Divine Spirit to provide the uniting third.

CHAPTER 14

THE IMPLANTED WORD — KNOWING FROM WITHIN:

James 1:17–27

Healing growth begins as we remember the Divine word that is implanted in us. When we recognize that our human personality houses the Divine, we begin to respect all that comes from within us. We trust the flow of our libido (life force); we relate to it as a harbinger of the larger Self/God Within. Mary and Joseph acted on guidance that came only to them. They did not have the affirmation of the outside world. They trusted their experience.

Verse 21, "Therefore rid your selves of all sordidness and rank growth of wickedness, and welcome with meekness the implanted word that has the power to save your souls."

WHAT GROWS from inside you? What are you aware of that is innate, inborn? What has been with you since birth? Often, people say, "I've always been like this" or "I've been like this ever since I can remember." Our family might agree, "You've always been like that."

Usually, these comments are made in reference to a behavior or personality trait that seems entrenched in our ways. It also might refer to a talent or disposition (interest, work, art) that has been evident from childhood.

Our sense of self, who we are, develops from the interplay of our inner world and the outer environment (including people). Life-giving and life-destroying ways arise from the interactions. The writer of James reminds us that we have the "implanted word that has the power to save your soul(s)." Within us, we have what is needed to move us away from the ways of feeling, thinking, and acting that are destructive.

I love the esoteric concept of "word." Words encapsulate consciousness; consciousness is the electromagnetic energy of the life force. It's an abstract concept, but very real. Just think about certain word phrases and note the differing images, sensations, and emotions they evoke. The "word" harnesses a state of consciousness that is evoked when we hear it. The words we use are important because they set in motion the energy of consciousness (the life force) they represent. James must have known of this. He reminds us to "bridle (our) tongues (and not) deceive (our) hearts."

The words of our self-talk shape our relationship to self. The attitudes, repetitive phrases, and momentary assessments shape our feelings of worth and value. How do you respond to yourself when pressured, challenged, off center, or not knowing? These are the times we are apt to launch into self-attack: "Stupid! You never get anything right! You always mess up! You're not gonna' ever have what you want!"

When we have such demeaning attitudes towards our selves, we tend towards haughtiness and judgment of others. The degree to which we are arrogant is the degree to which we feel worthless. The arrogance is displaced feelings of badness.

We need to monitor our self-talk. When curses, demeaning comments, and hateful attitudes arise, we need to look for the part of our self that needs tending. Tending to self brings healing, learning, and growth.

Healing growth begins as we remember the Divine word that is implanted in us. We recognize that our human personality houses the Divine. We can then change the negative self-talk. We can cultivate self-talk that affirms our innate value, worth, abilities, and being. Instead of the negatives stated above, we extend understanding to our selves. We look at what happened to find the seed of the Divine Self that is God's unique expression in that state of consciousness.

For instance, we may feel a "killer rage." We want to cut someone off, "rip them a new one," "rake them over the coals," or pummel them to death. We can fume, rant, and rave! Or, we can view what is deemed sordid and wicked with an eye toward seeing the organizing impulse or desire that is innate. In the case of the "killer rage," we would track the events and inner feeling responses that led up to it. We would use the energy of the rage to take the life-giving action called for in the situation. We would respond to it from our connection to the Self/God Within (the implanted word). △

Inner Reflection

How do you affirm God Within/the Self? What attitudes reflect your God-given value, worth, and innate abilities? How do you shape your self-esteem?

I invite you to track your relationship to yourself over the next 24 hours. Pay attention to how you respond to your inner and outer experiences. Where do you extend compassion and love? Where do you move into fear and self-degradation? Where do you know yourself to be connected to the Inner Divine? Where do you miss the connection? Cultivate an attitude of compassion and strength to all within you, as it is an expression of the inner Divine.

CHAPTER 15

SPEAKING UP:
Job 7:1–21

Job seemed to know that the distress of mind and bitterness of soul he was feeling was not all there was for him. He did not know what to do of his own accord to change it. He called out to God for help. Throughout the Christmas story, we see God's guidance. We can only imagine how many conversations Mary and Joseph must have had with God along the way. We too need to speak up. The Divine Within accompanies us through all.

Verse 11, "But I will not hold my peace; I will speak out in the distress of my mind, and complain in the bitterness of my soul."

WHERE do you give up and resign yourself to what is, even though you feel distress and bitterness of mind and soul? Where do you sink into passivity and inertia and feel put upon by others, including God? When Job was having more than his fair share of bad things happen to him, he chose not to suffer passively. He disavowed the role of compliant martyr, or "accepting his lot in life," and made a choice to "not hold (his) peace." He gave voice to his feelings and thoughts; he spoke out to himself, his friends, and God.

The book of Job has created much confusion for people. Why would God give over a loyal servant to be tested through suffering and loss? Whatever the answer, I believe that Job's choice to speak out and talk with God is an important example for us. We are gifted with the capacity for consciousness, and consciousness brings the capacity for dialogue in relationship. Job reminds us to use and strengthen our consciousness.

From the perspective of Jungian psychology, we can view the interaction between Job and God as representative of interaction between our ego/self and the Self/God Within. Our ego/self is our conscious sense of who we are; the Self/God Within is the whole of who we are. The Self, in its totality, holds our soul in all its expressions—instinctive, reflexive, learned, innate potentialities, etc. We are always more than the momentary self we know in one experience or set of circumstances.

Job seemed to know that the distress of mind and bitterness of soul he was feeling was not all there was for him. He was not willing to act as if it was. He gave voice to his feeling and called out for something more life sustaining. We have the same option. We, with our ego/self, can verbalize and dialogue with our larger Self, wherever we are. With consciousness, we can courageously see our distress and bitterness, and name it. In doing this, we begin to see the truth of where we are. We can open to the reality of the larger Self and call forth the desired and needed life-giving energies that can move us out of distress and bitterness into peace and joy.

Inner Reflection

I invite you to take a few minutes to name and give voice (verbally and/or on paper) to any "distress of (your) mind… or bitterness of (your) soul." Where are the negatives that block your libido (life force) from flowing freely? Where have you knowingly or unknowingly become complacent and accepted inertia as your norm?

Invite the courage of your soul to help you "not hold (your) peace" in these places. Call on the Inner Divine Spirit to come to you in your thoughts, feelings, intuitions, and sensations. Be willing to move into a life-giving and life-sustaining place (inner and outer).

CHAPTER 16

A NEW HEAVEN AND EARTH:
Revelation 21:1–8

The birth of Jesus over 2,000 years ago changed the world. When we allow our selves to give birth to our heart's desires, our worlds are changed. Receiving and trusting the new allows us to know the Divine in our lives.

Verses 1, 6, "Then I saw a new heaven and a new earth, for the first heaven and the first earth had vanished, and there was no longer any sea….[God said] I am the Alpha and the Omega, the beginning and the end. A draught from the water-springs of life will be my free gift to the thirsty."

THE VISION of John recorded in the book of Revelation is considered apocalyptic literature as it presents imagery of the end of the known world and the emergence of a new world. The "end of times" has evoked much speculation and many emotions as people wonder what it means to our earth community. Perhaps, we are better served when we consider the scripture symbolically as a metaphor for what happens to a person as he/she individuates.

Jung described individuation as an instinctive process whereby we move towards living more congruently from the Self/God Within. This means separating from the learned roles, adaptive responses, and habit patterns that are rote and out of sync with the truth of our soul. We must acknowledge and release the "should, must, and ought to" injunctions that take authority away from the Inner Divine Spirit.

The destruction of old ways of thinking, feeling, emoting, sensing, and perceiving has a ripple effect. The inner changes translate into attitudes, ways of interacting, choices, and behavioral responses that alter our being in the world. As a result, our relationships, surroundings, and circumstances change.

The "new heaven and a new earth" are symbols of the new thoughts, beliefs, mental processes, reflective responses, cellular patterns, instinctive urges, and behaviors that emerge as we consciously choose to align with the Self/God Within. Anyone who has courageously acted on the guidance of the Inner Divine Spirit to make changes in ways of being with self, Self/God Within, and others has experienced the destruction of the old world and the emergence of the new.

Destruction is always messy and anxiety provoking, at the least! If we reflect on tumultuous changes that have occurred in our lives, we can appreciate the sensational images that surround "the end of time." The unexpected positives, as well as the negatives, can upset the status quo and balance of our lives. Divorces, marriages, births, deaths, job changes, and geographical moves are just a few of the life events that demand inner shifts and a new world order. When we make changes that flow from the Inner Divine Spirit, the source of life, the Divine Within, sustains us.

The scripture reads, "[God said], A draught from the water-springs of life will be my free gift to the thirsty." The water of life is an ancient and powerful symbol of our libido, or life force, through which the Divine manifests in us. The "water-springs of life" is a beautiful image of the Self, the point of connection to God within our psyches. When we draw strength and compassion from the Self, a deep sense of inner peace sustains us through outer turmoil, changes, and difficult emotions. The path of individuation, as well as many spiritual disciplines, cultivates the connection between Self/God Within and ego so that the connection is readily accessible. This is the gift of the Self/God Within to those who seek.

Inner Reflection

Consider the state of your "heaven and earth." Create a picture with images or words that reflect the feeling tone of the physical, emotional, mental, and spiritual aspects of your life at this time. Note what is old, worn out, or destructive to you and your life. Celebrate what is new and life giving. Ask the Inner Divine to show you the next step in leaving the old, life-destroying ways and receiving and living more fully the ways of the new. Be courageous in seeing, receiving, and moving!

CHAPTER 17

THE DIVINE IS HERE:
John 20:1–18

The Self/God Within stands behind, or within, every experience of our body, mind, and psyche/soul. We have only to look with eyes that see the seed of the Divine that has taken shape within us and around us. All who encountered the Christ Child looked with eyes to see the unexpected.

Verses 13-14, Verses 13–14, "She answered, 'They have taken my Lord away, and I do not know where they have laid him.' With these words she turned round and saw Jesus standing there, but did not recognize him."

All has its rightful place.
The me that is Divine is right here
All I have to do is to turn around
To see outside the tomb
Of old memories and past experiences
To roll away the blocks to this moment

The caves of hiding must be left
There is a time to walk into the open
To move from the womb of the old
To the free flowing light
Where life grows and moves again

All that is dead will be reborn
It's just a matter of time
Forgotten desires find outlets
Denied emotions inform our actions
The Self we lost returns

We must roll the stone away
Push back the blocks to our path
Follow the thread of our heart
To know the truth of what is
We see the Divine in this moment

WE ENCOUNTER THE Divine every moment, yet we often do not recognize our Lord. We are created in the image of God, so our body and mind are reflections of Divine energy. We meet God in every breath. Each breath infuses our cellular consciousness with Divine Essence. Our body communicates this essence to us with sensation and emotion. Our mind, meaning our intellect and desire nature working in tandem, informs us through image and word. The Divine becomes flesh in us.

We may not see the Divine, including our Self (God Within), in the present moment because we deem "what is" mundane, undesirable, wrong. "What is" may not fit our description of what Divine looks like. The institutional church has historically devalued the body. The flesh was deemed problematic at best, demonic at worst. Such preconceived ideas, dismissal of our experiences, devaluing of our selves, and deferring to outer authority block our ability to receive the Self's communications.

Mary Magdalene did not expect to see Jesus standing outside the tomb. Although she was looking for him, she did not see him initially. He was in a place and a form (body) she did not expect. She knew he had been crucified; she came looking for his tomb. Her expectations and previous experience interfered with her seeing Christ when she first saw him outside the tomb.

Like Mary Magdalene, we often do not see the Divine at first glance. Our beliefs and our history can be a fortress that creates tunnel vision. We all have learned patterns of response to our selves—our embodied experiences of sensations, emotions, intuitions, thoughts, and feelings. We have patterns of moving in relationship to our selves and others based on historical realities. These patterns are problematic because the present moment is not the historical one. Too often, we unwittingly live the past instead of the present. We are not able to see beyond the unconscious restraints of what has been.

Mary Magdalene's encounter with a risen Christ reminds us that we can move beyond our preconceived ideas and history. The Self/God Within stands behind, or within, every experience of our body, mind, and psyche/soul. We have only to look for the unexpected. To look with eyes that see the seed of the Divine that has taken shape within us.

△

Inner Reflection

Begin looking at all within you as a cloaked seed of the Self/God Within. Look beyond your initial reactions to see the deeper essence of what is. If it is a negative feeling, idea, or fantasy, what is the seed energy? Hold the negative in the context of the whole and invite the deeper essence to show itself to you.

CHAPTER 18

COMING INTO THE LIGHT:
1 John 2:1–11

Jung stated, "We do not become conscious by imagining figures of Light. We become conscious by bringing Light to the Darkness." Our willingness to relate to our dark feelings and the unknown stirrings within us is key for transformation. The seasons of Advent and Epiphany occur when we experience the shortest sun-filled days. This is the time we celebrate the birth of the Christ. The birth of the Divine within us occurs at the moments of greatest darkness.

Verses 9–11, "A man may say, 'I am in the light,' but if he hates his brother, he is still in the dark. Only the man who loves his brother dwells in the light: there is nothing to make him stumble. But one who hates his bother is in darkness; he walks in the dark and has no idea where he is going, because the darkness has made him blind."

A GIFT OF BEING HUMAN is our ability to see the inner workings within our selves and to see beyond surface appearances in the outer world. With our physical eyes and senses, we take in outside impulses and experience sensory data that yield perceptions.

Our animal nature or automatic consciousness responds reflexively to the data based on patterned responses from past experiences that include our life history and biology/instincts. Acting reflexively is like being in

60

the dark. No conscious, observing self is intervening or mediating the response. We are acting from tunnel vision, limited in the moment by the automatic pattern. We lack the vision to see the whole of who we are beyond the momentary experience

Vision always comes as Light. We equate Light with Consciousness. Consciousness by definition means there is an awareness and connection to our sense of self or ego—our known experience or "I am." The counterpart of consciousness is unconsciousness. The unconscious is that which is unknown and usually appears as unbidden body sensations, desires, images or fleeting thoughts or fantasies. The contents of the unconscious often feel chaotic and non-rational as they are not connected to or controlled by our sense of self. We feel as if we are in the dark.

To be in the Light requires following the "new command"

or spiritual law to "Love your neighbor." We must begin within our selves. If our egos, or who we are, hate and detest what is in us—thoughts, feelings, desires—we stay in the dark. When we begin to love those parts of our selves we deem ugly, immoral, even sinful, we can see what these parts have been trying to help us see about our nature.

Seeds of the Divine Within are often cloaked in unhelpful patterns of response conditioned during our early lives when we were dependent and helpless. By seeing the seed of the Divine that has been fleshed out in a distorted way, we open the door for the Divine essence to grow in a different way. The essence is freed to take shape in a new feeling, impulse, or desire that yields new life-giving, light-bringing behavior. In this way, we come into the Light.

$\triangle$

Inner Reflection

I invite you to sit today with those undesired or problematic aspects of yourself and practice the law of Love. Ask to see the true essence of the Divine Nature in the darkness and to be moved into the Light.

CHAPTER 19

MOVING OUT OF THE CAVES:
1 Kings 19:1–15a

There is a time of retreat when we are giving birth to new life. The new life may show up as a creative project, a love relationship, different interests, or healthier habits. There is also a retreat that is an avoidance of living. Our anxieties about not being all-powerful or in control can trigger withdrawal that stops our growth. We fear encountering the unknown Mystery. The story of Elijah reminds us to stay present to what is; it may be the stirrings of the Divine.

Verses 11-13, "The answer came: 'Go stand on the mount before the Lord.' For the Lord was passing by: a great and strong wind came rending mountains and shattering rocks before him, but the Lord was not in the earthquake; and after the earthquake fire, but the Lord was not in the fire; and after the fire a low murmuring sound…Then there came a voice."

NOW OFTEN do we retreat to the caves of silence, withdrawal, or preoccupation with media or projects, those invisible walls between others and us or between our larger Self and us?

In today's passage, the prophet Elijah had retreated to a cave in fear for his life. We, like Elijah, get afraid. We fear that interaction with others or some not fully known part of our Selves will destroy us. So, we retreat; we numb, go unconscious, get confused, stay with unknowing.

The beauty of Biblical stories is they remind us of psychological as well as spiritual truths. The way out of the fear and out of the cave is standing before the Self/God Within. The Self/God Within always seeks us out and calls us to reconnect and to listen. This requires moving out of the caves, beyond the invisible emotional and mental walls that separate us from our Inner Divine Spirit and other people.

When Elijah is called to stand before the Lord, he witnesses an earthquake and a fire and a low murmuring sound. The voice of God is not in these acts of destruction, but Elijah must witness them before hearing the voice of God. Symbolically, the earthquake and fire represent phases of transformation.

We have all experienced symbolic earthquakes, the moments when the ground of our beliefs, ideas, self-perceptions, ways of interacting, and outer world relationships have shifted. Familiar, comfortable, and old ways of being with our selves and others have been shattered. The moments of symbolic fire occur when our anger or passions rage and we know something must change internally and externally.

Our willingness to stand and see the elements of transformation at work in us and around us precedes hearing the voice of God. We must face the necessary destruction of what is in order to hear the voice of God Within and have new life.

Inner Reflection

What are your caves? How do the physical, emotional, mental, and spiritual walls between you and the Self/God Within look? Where and how do they appear between you and other people? Open yourself to hear the Inner Divine Spirit calling you to move out of the caves and to see what needs to be seen. Ask for courage to withstand the earthquakes and fires of transformation so you may hear the voice of God Within.

CHAPTER 20

MOVING INTO THE NEW:
Acts 18:12–28

For new life to emerge, old ways have to move aside. This story from Acts is symbolic of the internal processes of resistance to the new. We see this in the Christmas story where Herod wanted the baby Jesus killed. Mary and Joseph protected the Christ child by taking an alternative route home. We too have to protect the new bits of Self from the attitudes that seek to destroy it.

Verses 15b-16, "Gallio said to them....'I have no mind to be a judge in these matters.' And he had them ejected from the court. Then there was a general attack on Sosthenes, who held office in the synagogue, and they gave him a beating in full view of the bench. But all this left Gallio quite unconcerned."

THE STORY from Acts tells about the Roman proconsul Gallio's response to the Jews who brought Paul before Gallio on charges Paul was "inducing people to worship God in ways that are against the law" (verse 14). The events that play out symbolize the violence that can go on inside us when something new, outside the established law, emerges.

The "law" represents the learned ways of sensing, feeling, thinking, and emoting that we internalize from the outside world. In the story, the Jews symbolize the inner authority that is modeled after the collective consciousness. The collective consciousness includes attitudes and beliefs of our culture, society, and institutions, including church and school, community, and family. These collective attitudes and beliefs become the "norm" and the "expected." This "norm" shows up in rote ways of living. We know it is at work when we say: "We just don't do that!" "We don't talk about those things!" "We never act like that!"

The collective becomes the "old guard—adaptive, learned ways that become entrenched and self-protective. The voices of inner judgment that say, "You should, you ought to, you must," are agents of the old authority that hold us to compliance with the norms. Think of how these voices have blocked the flow and expression of an innate impulse in you even today!

Paul represents a new attitude, a new way of being, feeling, and experiencing the Divine.

With the appearance of the new, we begin to move differently. We choose to act on the desires of our heart. We listen for the voice of the Inner Divine Spirit. We replace the learned, adaptive patterns with thoughts, feelings, and actions that more accurately express our soul's desires.

As the old (symbolized by the Jews) feels threatened, it presents its argument to the ego, symbolized by Gallio, as to why the new (Paul) is doing something wrong. We experience this whenever the inner established ways feel challenged and threatened. Think of your reflexive resistance when someone innocently offers an idea or view you have not considered. The dynamic is also at work where we want to change a behavior but keep repeating the old behavior. Arguments emerge that rationalize and justify the lack of change and growth.

Gallio represents the ego when it does not take responsibility for mediating the energies (feelings, emotions, thoughts, intuitions, sensations) that are in conflict within us. Think about times when we say, "I just don't want to deal with that now." We know something problematic is brewing internally, but we dismiss it as Gallio dismissed Paul and the Jews.

When we refuse to exercise our consciousness to discern the truth of our inner experiences, we open the door to violence towards our selves. Violence towards the self/Self shows up as feelings of self-hate, shame, and criticism; self-destructive behaviors; illnesses and other body symptoms; self-demeaning attitudes, etc.

The old ways turn on us when we refuse to make a choice to stand by the new life-giving energies. In the story, "there was a general attack on Sosthenes…and (the Jews) gave him a beating in full view of the bench." All we are told about Sosthenes is that he is an officer in the synagogue. He has some power in the system. In our psyches, he may show up as a bridging idea, an open mind-edness, a different perception, or a longing or desire. Regardless of the form, "Sosthenes" is given a beating.

Inner Reflection

Take a few minutes to reflect on your inner conflicts. Where is the ego refusing to mediate between old and new ways of being, experiencing, expressing? Where are you beating yourself?

Feel into the attacked places and invite the old and new ideas, feelings, etc. to show themselves. Explore the feeling nuances of each and identify the beliefs and experiences behind each. Ask the Inner Divine Spirit to grant you courage and discernment to face and mediate the conflict.

CHAPTER 21

OUT WITH THE OLD AND IN WITH THE NEW
Colossians 3:1–17

Epiphany means we have had a sudden realization of God. We wake up to the Divine presence in a new way. We cannot make our selves have an epiphany, but we can cultivate ways of being that facilitate seeing the Divine. The starting point is working with our emotional natures. When we seek the connection to the Self/God Within in whatever we are experiencing, we open to an epiphany.

Verses 87, 12, 14, "But now you must your selves lay aside all anger, passion, malice, cursing, filthy talk— have done with them!...Then put on the garments that suit God's chosen people, his own, his beloved: compassion, kindness, humility, gentleness, patience… To crown all, there must be love, to bind all together and to complete the whole."

"TO LAY ASIDE"and "to put on" indicate that we have the ability to respond and to relate to our emotions and feelings with will—or the capacity to choose how to behave. To have choice, we must have an aware- ness of our internal stirrings that prompt our thoughts and actions. We must see and relate to what is going on behind our emotional states.

Every emotional state has a message about our experience. For instance, when we feel angry, we want something to be different. We have a sense that something needs to change. Usually, we interpret this sense to mean someone or something else needs to change! However, it is our response that psyche is prompting us to shift.

Cursing and filthy talk often mask feelings of disgust and an identification with old, worn-out, lifeless experiences and emotions. Instead of our life force flowing forward and outward into thoughts, words, and behaviors, it is thwarted and implodes in our internal experience. We need to free the life force so we can use it in service of life. Becoming aware or conscious of automatic, conditioned responses is the first step towards mediating them.

This mediation requires a relationship and a dialogue. Two parties, sometimes wanting different things, must sit down together and talk. An exchange occurs. Much unbidden and undirected dialogue goes on in our heads. We can begin an inner dialogue with our emotions, feelings, or sensations at anytime. Such dialogue forges conscious connection to our Divine Nature/the Self that allows us to transcend/rise above the immediate state of consciousness. This is what it means to be raised to new life in Christ.

We have to remember that our momentary sense of self and experience is not all there is. The Self or Divine Within wants to be called on and invited to shift our internal experience to the whole of who we are. Our conscious invitation through paying attention to the emotion, talking with the emotion, and getting to know the message of the emotion frees the energy in us so that we can lay aside what is not needed, and "put on" what is needed. The writer of Colossians tells us, "love…bind(s) all together and complete(s) the whole."

Inner Reflection

Take a few minutes to consider the emotions listed in the scripture verses above. Be open to seeing where the emotions are surfacing during this time in your life and what they are saying to you. Practice meeting yourself, your inner experience, with compassion, kindness, humility, gentleness, and patience! Allow love to help you experience and know the whole of your Inner Divine Spirit.

CHAPTER 22

LET THE OLD DIE AND THE NEW GROW:
Nehemiah 1:1–11

For Joseph to wed Mary, he had to let go of his preconceived ideas. Mary's pregnancy before marriage was not the "right" cultural norm. Joseph trusted his encounter with the Divine. He set aside the old beliefs and acted with his heart. We too must let the old go in order to move forward with the new that is life giving.

Verse 4, "When I heard this news, I sat down and wept; I mourned for some days, fasting and praying to the God of heaven."

OUR CULTURE has a penchant for making everything light, bright, and happy. The hedonistic mentality of pleasure in the moment, no matter what, leaves no place for the necessary periods of grieving and mourning that are a part of the cycle of life. We forget that for something new to come, something old must go.

The season of fall teaches us the necessity of the old dying and letting go in order for new growth to come. As the beautiful, colorful leaves fall to the ground, the bud of the leaf that is coming pushes the dead away. By letting go, the dead makes space for the new to appear.

To grow, we must be willing to let go of "that which no longer grows us corn"—old deadening habits, thought patterns, beliefs, relationships, pursuits, emotional expectations, etc. Sometimes, the dead is attached to family, institutional, or cultural traditions. What was once beautiful and healthy and life giving, just like the green leaves of spring, has changed colors and is dying. The season and time for that way of being with our selves, family, friends, coworkers, and world has passed. These aspects of the Self must change/die.

We know what is dying by the stench it creates. The stench manifests in numerous ways. Physically, we may become ill, have accidents, persist in self-destructive behaviors, or experience increasing muscle tension. Emotionally, we may feel angry, resentful, bitter, apathetic, or stifled. Mentally, we may obsess, zone out, numb, or stay in fantasy. Spiritually, we may align with fear, go into "overdrive" as if we were omnipotent, or

become depressed. Unlike trees, we humans can block the emergence of new life by holding on to what is known. The stench is the result!

It is an act of courage, and a necessary step in individuation, to consciously let go of ways of being that block living the truth of that which you know from God Within. (Individuation is Jung's term for the process of letting go of the learned ways of being that block embodying and consciously living in relationship to God Within/the Self).

As we willingly grow, we experience loss and we feel sad. Grief shows up with its stages of denial, anger, bargaining, depression, and acceptance. Consciously feeling and moving through these emotions allow us to clear our psychic space. The clearing creates a fertile void in which the new can grow.

Inner Reflection

I invite you to identify what in your life is dead or dying. Look in every plane—physical, emotional, mental, and spiritual. Become willing to consciously let go of the old and to receive the new. Grieve and mourn the loss, and GROW! With every leaf you see falling today, ask your Inner Divine Spirit to help you let go and remember the new is coming!

CHAPTER 24

KEEPING COVENANT:
2 Kings 17:24–41

We think of the birth of the Christ as God's new covenant to his people. Every time a new aspect of our larger Self, or God Within, emerges, we are called to live in covenant to the Divine in our nature. Covenant means relationship. Relationship means dialogue. We keep covenant with our Self/God Within by engaging with all aspects of our self.

Verses 39-39, "You shall not forget the covenant which I made with you; you shall not pay homage to other gods. But to the Lord your God you shall pay homage, and he will preserve you from all your enemies."

HERE'S ONE of my favorite stories from the Kabbalah: At the moment of our conception, we were given a Holy Guardian Angel who accompanied us in the womb. The Holy Guardian Angel shared all the secrets of the universe and our life's purpose with us. At the moment of birth, we forgot it all! We spend our life trying to connect back to what we know but have forgotten. The Kabbalistic tradition teaches that the Holy Guardian Angel is the Self (God Within). The Self is the organizing principle of our psyche/soul and is the totality of our psyche. All energies we experience within our selves are aspects of the Self.

The Self can be viewed as an expression or extension of Yahweh. The ego/self is an expression or extension of the

Self. From this perspective, the scripture stated above speaks symbolically of the need for the ego/self to remember its covenant with the Self.

Covenant implies a relationship between two parties. From a Jungian psychological perspective, the ego builds a relationship with the Self by tending that which is emerging, expressing spontaneously, not yet fully known. Often the unconscious Self shows up as an unbidden and unexpected affect in waking life or in dreams. (An affect is an emotion-laden state of consciousness.) Affective moods can feel like "gods" to us!

The "gods" referenced in the Old Testament are symbols of archetypes. Archetypes are numinous energies that we first experience as a feeling. There are limitless numbers of archetypes. They manifest in us as feelings or moods that prompt impulses, desires, and images specific to the archetype. For instance, the following arche-

types each possess a unique felt quality: Mother, Father, Creator, Destroyer, Lover, King, and Magician. It is the ego's responsibility to meet the affective "gods" and help them find their rightful place and expression.

We can discern our covenant with the Self, the direction of our libido/life force, by mediating the archetypal energies of our affects, impulses, and desires. Sometimes, we get "carried away" by emotions and feelings and act in ways that are not congruent to the totality of who we are. People sometimes say, "I don't know what got into me!" when they behave "out of character." Other times, we knowingly engage in behaviors that are self-destructive and undesired (such as, passivity, overeating, promiscuity, or over-drinking).

Many Old Testament stories highlight Yahweh's demand to be honored as the only God. Psychologically, the Self makes the same demand. We experience a sense of peace and well being when the ego is aligned with the Self, and we suffer when the ego acts separately in service to an unmediated affect or archetype/"god." △

Inner Reflection

Take a few minutes to reflect on your relationship to your Self. Feel into the place where you know the "Holy Guardian Angel." Ask for clarity and direction about the archetypes/affective states with which you are currently struggling. Be willing to see where and how you need to align with the Self/God Within. Be willing to consciously know and integrate the energies in service of the Inner Divine Spirit.

PARABLE OF THE TALENTS—USE WHAT YOU HAVE:

Matthew 25:14–30, Luke 19:12–27

In the Christmas story, the innkeeper was creative in finding space for Mary and Joseph. He did not have a room in the end, so he offered them the stable. It was what he had, and he chose to use it. We can thwart the birth of the Divine in our life by not using what we have. The Parable of the Talents reminds us to risk using what we have even when it does not seem enough.

I LED A SEMINAR where we had a lot of discussion about having. People struggled with feelings of guilt about having, questions of deserving ("Why should I have when others don't have?"), embarrassing experiences, and shame in relationship to other's jealousy and envy towards them. Ideas about limitations, choices, powerlessness, personal choice, freedom of movement, and victimhood circled in our midst. I thought of The Parable of the Talents and what it might tell us.

We have four characters in the story, with each character representing an energy or state of consciousness in our psyche/ soul and bodymind. The story offers a picture of how the energies work together within us. When we see this interaction of energies, we, with our ego consciousness, are able to better manage and use the energies. The energies show up in our physical, emotional, mental, and spiritual bodies. We have impulses, emotions, beliefs, desires, passions, etc. All hold consciousness. Consciousness (from the Kabbalistic view) is synonymous with the life force or chi that holds the essence of the Divine. Life force flows through us in our breath; all that results in our body is ultimately dependent on the breath as it connects us to Spirit.

The rich man in the parable may be viewed as symbolic of the Self, the totality of psyche/soul. The Self is the psychic structure that holds all of who we are and what we experience together. It is the vessel that receives, contains, and shapes the Divine essence that is the spark of life in us. The Self is transcendent in that it can "reap where it does not sow."

The principle of synchronicity shows up for the Self. Things seems to happen and come together in a way the ego never imagined. Think about times in your life when something you deeply yearned for happened. Usually, unsolicited help, people, and circumstances were involved. When we receive and use the desires and beliefs of our heart, we are investing what the Self has given us.

The three servants represent different attitudes we can have towards the desires/energies we experience. *First and foremost, the sensations, intuitions, feelings, and thoughts of our body and mind are what we are given to manage.* We are so often like the third servant who hides the talent. We are afraid of the reactions or outcome of our choices, so we hide the impulse or desire. We do not act on it; we repress it, dismiss it, and disavow it! The energy does not go away. It remains hidden until something demands we access it.

Have you ever put off doing something you wanted/needed to do for yourself until you seemed to have no choice but to act? Often, this happens with dietary or other lifestyle changes! Usually, we have some negative condition, a physical illness, emotional distress, mental discord, and/or spiritual unrest, that finally prompts change. We experience "being thrown out into the street with the darkness and gnashing of teeth." We feel lost, outside our selves. We need to reconnect with and act on the desire or impulse we have set aside. Remember, what we are given first is our bodymind. *We always have the resource of our embodiment— sensations (bodily feelings), intuitions (gut knowings), feelings (felt worth), and thoughts (assessments).*

The two servants who used the talents/monies affirm the right action of using what we are given. They took the talents (energies, heart's desires) they were given and created with the given talents. These two servants were willing to risk making choices and taking action.

The greatest gift we have is the vessel of our psyche/soul and body into which the Self pours itself. Through our embodied self, the Self/Divine Essence informs us. When our ego consciousness grasps, holds, cultivates, and acts on this truth, our lives become fuller, richer, more whole, and always forward moving. We experience joy! As the two servants who acted with the talents, we are invited into the Master's house for celebration. We are more whole, more resourceful, and more alive! We are given more!

Inner Reflection

Take a few minutes to reflect on where you are like the servants. Where are you hiding your talents/energies? Where are you investing and cultivating your desires? How is the Self prompting you? What is growing? What is dying? Set sacred intention to act on what you know to be true in your heart for your soul. Practice a discipline (like meditation or journaling) that helps you become more aware of your felt experience. Access whatever resources you need to free your energies to move towards life.

CREATING CONSCIOUSNESS:
Genesis 32:22–31

The story of Jacob wrestling with the angel is in contrast to the seemingly easy encounter of the angels with Mary and Joseph. At times in our journey we are given the blessing of conscious knowing effortlessly. At other times we have to want the light of consciousness and fight for it. Our tenacity in holding onto our desire is what brings us the blessing.

Luke 19: 20-21, "The third came and said, 'here is your pound, sir; I kept it put away in a handkerchief. I was afraid of you, because you are a hard man; you draw out what you never put in and reap what you did not sow."

I HEARD A SERMON preached about what a scoundrel Jacob was. Jacob had a way of going after and getting what he wanted even when it meant cheating and taking from another. The presenter stated that in Hebrew Jacob means "one who grabs; a usurper." I immediately thought about Prometheus. In Greek mythology, Prometheus stole fire from the gods and gave it to humans.

Both Jacob and Prometheus saw something they valued and wanted, and they grabbed it.

In today's scripture, Jacob wanted the blessing of the angel with whom he wrestled. He was not willing to let go until he had it! Previously, he had wanted his brother Esau's birthright. When Esau wanted food Jacob had prepared, Jacob demanded the birthright in exchange for the meal. Esau readily agreed. What

Esau saw as meaningless in the moment, Jacob grabbed! When their father was dying, Jacob craftily tricked his father into passing the firstborn blessing to Jacob.

Prometheus and Jacob went for the spirit (fire) that would carry and sustain them. They intentionally and consciously pursued what created more consciousness and life. With their actions, they valued what had energy and grabbed what carried the life force/libido. Esau did not. He sold his birthright for a meal! He did not hold onto what mattered—an inheritance that would sustain him and those closest to him.

Symbolically, fire is consciousness. The Divine Spirit is often depicted as tongues of fire. The creative life force pulsing through our bodies and souls can be described as "a fire that requires no wood." It just burns!

I believe this is what Jacob felt and sought as he grabbed for the blessings of his father and the angel.

Jung has described consciousness as *contra naturem* (against nature). To have a self that has choice, and does not just respond automatically and reflexively from instincts or learned patterns of experience, requires effort. We have to work to build a relationship between what we know about our selves and what we do not know but do feel and experience. We have to want and seek something more than we have in our consciousness. Only when we value increased consciousness will our ego/self struggle to grab and hold onto the fiery energies of our heart and soul. We claim the blessing of "fire" that is our birthright as we wrestle with whatever comes to us.

Inner Reflection

Where are you wrestling within yourself? What are the sensations, feelings, thoughts, intuitions, perceptions, etc. that surround the struggle? Track what has the greatest fire or energy. Seek the blessing of consciousness that is present and let it give you the needed resources from within to create life-sustaining relationships and environs.

CHAPTER 26

FOLLOWING INNER DIVINE:
Genesis 27:30–45

Mary and Joseph broke with the customs of their day. She was pregnant out of wedlock; Joseph still chose to marry her. In the Genesis story, Jacob gets something out of order according to the customs of his day. Often, the Self/God Within calls us to step outside the familiar roles that restrict our heart's longings. New life means something changes. The new replaces the old.

Verse 41, "Esau bore a grudge against Jacob because of the blessing which his father had given him, and he said to himself, 'The time of mourning for my father will soon be here; then I will kill my brother Jacob.'"

The story of Esau and Jacob offers a look at the competition, trickery, and murderous desires that are present and active within our psyches. Symbolically, the first-born Esau may represent a way of experiencing and expressing self that is a response to the outside world. He represents the known order; he follows the established "rules and regulations" of the day. These rules include family, institutions, social mores, etc.

We can consider Esau our "adaptive" self. The adaptive self includes the ways we defend or distance from our felt sense or embodied experiences. The most common way of creating this distance is denial. We deny our emotions, feelings, needs, or desires to avoid negative responses from our selves or others.

Jacob, the twin who was second-born, represents something in us that moves with freedom from the restrictions of the known order. After birth, the first known social order is the family system into which we are born. The first-born way of being in the world is shaped here. Natural tendencies and inclinations toward expression are often sacrificed to fit in! Jacob represents an alternative way that, though born simultaneously, is not the favored way because it does not comply with the outer standards and expectations

Jacob and Esau represent inner conflict that is present in all of us. Rote, familiar ways conflict with alternative, less restrictive, and more life-giving ways. We have all experienced this when trying to change a habit pattern. We want something different, yet the old, established ways seem intent on destroying the new.

In the scripture story, Jacob has the blessing of his father and the aid of his mother. Symbolically, we can interpret this to mean that the alternative, non-familiar, natural way of being has the favor of the Self/God Within. The Inner Divine Spirit supports the life-giving desires and energies of our souls. When we look to the Self, we can find a way to bring the new, life-giving energy into being.

⋀

Inner Reflection

Take a few minutes to acknowledge any inner conflicts. Identify the learned, familiar pattern or response and the accompanying alternative way. What comes automatically (the first born) and what accompanies it (the twin that is second born)? Ask the Inner Divine Spirit to show you the way beyond the conflict.

CHAPTER 27

ONENESS OF BODY AND MIND:
2 Corinthians 5:6–10

The spiritual path of the West is Incarnation. The Christmas story celebrates God becoming man. The spiritual and the physical are one and the same; they are just different densities of the same energy. We encounter the Divine first in our embodied experiences. We have to learn to stay consciously aware of our body experience to know the Divine in the world.

Verses 5, 9-10, "Even though we know that while we are at home in the body we are away from the Lord—for we walk by faith, not by sight…we make it our aim to please him. For all of us must appear before the judgment seat of Christ, so that each may receive recompense for what has been done in the body, whether good or evil."

MANY PEOPLE think of the body/mind and Divine Spirit as opposites. Yet, the image of The Tree of Life, from the esoteric Judeo-Christian tradition found in Kabbalah, teaches they are one. The Limitless Light/essence of God flows into the Chaiah/Universal Life Force that takes shape in the Neshamah/the Divine Soul. Our individual souls flow from the Divine Soul and take shape in our personalities/bodies/minds. The body/mind is simply an extension of the Divine Essence within us.

Paul is noting the felt sense of natural (unconscious) humanity when he speaks of being in the body as "being away from the Lord." Natural humanity is not yet aware or conscious that the Divine Spirit is present and accessible beyond the surface appearances of sensory experience. In a state of natural humanity, we respond to our felt experience as if it were the absolute truth.

With consciousness, we begin to see with our inner eyes the essence within the experience/form and know the movement of the Life Force within the form. We recognize there are many possibilities for how the Life Force or Limitless Light takes shape in us. We name its various expressions as our sensations, emotions, intuitions, thoughts, feelings, etc.

We open to experience the Divine within these states by holding the following thoughts: Our body/mind experiences express our Divine Spirit. Our Divine Spirit gives form to our body/mind experiences. The act of seeking to know this connection acknowledges that the Divine is present. Our body experiences, or embodiment, are opportunities to experience and know God in our very being. We open to faith.

Faith can be defined as the result of a supraconscious (beyond ego, transcendent) experience that we cannot put into adequate words. Yet, we are touched and changed by it forever. We cannot make our selves have faith, but we can open to receive faith experiences by seeking to know the Divine Within, "to please him."

To please the Divine Within, we must honor and respond to our felt sense experiences as they are connected to our Inner Divine Spirit. Impulsive responses or automatic sensations and emotions are present because they express an aspect of the Divine Within. The Divine expresses through all our feeling states, even those ugly, negative ones we learned to dismiss. We have to ask what the seed of the felt sense wants us to see and know about our selves/our souls.

Paul says that we receive "recompense for what has been done in the body." Webster's definition of recompense includes "to return in kind: requite; an equivalent or a return for something done, suffered, or given." Recompense operates in the psychological and spiritual law of compensation. Conscious compensates unconscious; unconscious compensates conscious. Body and mind compensate the unseen, but felt, energetic essence that we are. Our Life Force compensates the body and mind. Our embodied experiences are expressions of our Inner Divine Spirit. We may think or act as if the two are opposed and split, but this error creates much suffering and alienation from the Divine Within.

Inner Reflection

Reflect on how recent embodied experiences, pleasant and unpleasant, are expressing the flow of your Life Force. Look for what your Inner Divine Spirit is saying through your sensory experience. What is being returned in kind between your thoughts and feelings and between your sensations and intuitions? Ask to receive faith that you may know the oneness of your body/mind and your Inner Divine Spirit.

CHAPTER 28

LIVING THE TRUTH OF WHO YOU ARE:
Deuteronomy 3:1–11

When the Christ child was born, old allegiances had to be broken. The wise men did not return to Herod as instructed. Mary and Joseph went home differently than planned. We have to willingly destroy the ways of being and doing that stop us from living the truth of our true Self.

Verse 6, "Thus we put to death all the men, women, and dependents in every city, as we did Sihon king of Heshbon. All the cattle and the spoil from the cities we took as booty for our selves."

MANY OLD Testament stories tell of Israel's advance into Canaan and the destruction of foreign cultures and peoples. If we consider the stories symbolically and psychologically, we see the proper use of destructive energies—to destroy what in our natures is not in alignment with our Inner Divine Spirit. Where we have inner conflicts, we are called to clarify the desires of our heart and soul.

Jesus states, "Thou cannot serve two masters."

The Divine Within/Self demands that we sacrifice/give up the ways of being and expressing that are not true to our innate nature. Living in sync with the Self/the totality of psyche is a requirement on the path known spiritually as salvation or enlightenment and psychologically as individuation.

Jung states that every person's libido has a gradient (direction) it will naturally follow. Emotional, mental, and physical problems result when the natural flow of our Spirit is thwarted or distorted. Disturbances show us where we are not living true to our life force.

Thwarting of our soul's impulses and desires happens inadvertently as we are socialized to live according to expectations of family, church, school, culture, etc. Tempering of primitive impulses (that is, all the things the Ten Commandments prohibit—stealing, killing, etc.) is necessary to healthy and civilized living. The tempering is problematic only when expressions of our nature wrongly get tied to these prohibitions as we are shamed, guilted, or hurt because of what we have expressed.

Fear of the other—what is not us, not like our perceived self—fuels our rejection and dismissing of our desires. Balancing of our animal nature (including instincts noted in the Ten Commandments) occurs as we bring our instinctive impulses to light and see them in relationship to what we value and to present day realities.

For instance, we may feel so angry at another person that we think, "I could beat them to a pulp…I'm going to tear them apart (verbally)." As we see the impulse and hold it in the context of all we feel and desire—the larger whole of who we are that probably includes wanting to express love and care for self and other and not to be violent—we can free the energy of the anger for constructive use. This might mean a healthy and mutually respectful conversation happens, or we set needed boundaries, or we express the energy in an unrelated activity. People often talk about how much housework they get done when angry!

By freeing the energy, we take "the cattle and spoil…as booty." We intentionally use the motive power of the feeling-toned response in service of our Self/the whole of psyche or soul rather than the momentary experience of self/ego. The energies of creation, equilibrium, and destruction are always at work in us. For example, these energies are at work in our physical bodies in the processes of ingestion, digestion, and assimilation of food.

Inner Reflection

Think about how the energies of destruction, equilibrium, and creation are at work in you now. What are the forms—beliefs, values, habits, and behaviors—that are interfering with living the truth of who you are? What are your soul's desires that want to take shape—to be born or created in the world? Set an intention and practice to align with destroying that which is not true to your nature, creating (bringing into action/form) your heart's desires, and celebrating the beauty and balance of your Inner Divine Spirit.

APPENDIX
Meditation Summaries

1. Do Not Be Afraid:
Luke 1:26–38

We need to remember that the only true safety lies with the Self/God Within. When a new desire, emotion, impulse, or longing arises within us, we may feel afraid. These bits of Self are like the angel Gabriel. They announce new life is coming. Do not be afraid!

2. The Mystery of Darkness:
Job 23:1–9, 16–17

We are restored to health and vitality in life as we willingly engage the unknown, the darkness and mystery of the Self. What we fear seeing in ourselves almost always holds the key to greater living. The birth of the Christ child invites us to see beyond what we know and to willingly dialogue with parts of our nature that are problematic.

3. God Comes with Fire:
Psalm 50:3

Mary and Joseph journeyed a long way immediately before the birth of Jesus. We can only imagine the difficulties and turmoil they experienced. Often, the birth of something new in our life, inner and outer, is preceded by a shake up. The peace and calm we desire comes after we make room for the new aspect of our larger Self/God Within.

4. Letting Go of Form:
Exodus 32:21–34

Life starts from the Mystery of the Limitless Light, "the world without form and void." The birth of a baby always brings a world that is constantly changing. The old order is upset. It has to change. Our willingness to let go of the forms of how we used to be, what we used to do, etc. is necessary to grow the new life that comes.

5. Seeking God's Support Through the Self/God Within:
Galations 1:1–18

When we act in obeisance to the prevailing outer world standards, we often persecute parts of ourselves that are expressions of the Self/God Within. Our learned attitudes and beliefs may be threatened; we respond to the new with the violence of self-degradation, self-hatred, etc. Like Mary and Joseph and the wise men, we must chose to receive and act on the protective direction of the Self/God Within. Paul did this in response to his life-changing encounter with God.

6. Cycling—Opposites of Creation and Destruction:
Ecclesiastes 3:1–15

"He has made everything in its season." There is a time for birthing and a time for dying. We need to know how to align with the cycles of creation and destruction, to discern what is needed when. The larger Self/God Within guides us to know when we are willing to act on the guidance. Mary and Joseph acted on God's guidance even when it was inconvenient and socially awkward. They destroyed old conventions to give birth to the Christ.

7. Being Exposed:
Hebrews 4:11–16

When we encounter the Divine, we are seen. When we are seen, we are exposed. Nothing is hidden. We see truths about ourselves that we have avoided. We have to search ourselves to hold all the truths of our nature together. We can imagine that Mary and Joseph had to search their hearts multiple times as they lived the life–changing events of the Christ child being born. They had to choose to follow the Mystery. We, too, must search our hearts and chose to go with the birth of the Self/God Within as new aspects of ourselves show up.

8. A Revelry for New Life:
Luke 2:6–7

Nature has its own timing in the birthing process! When it's time to deliver, it's time. When something in our nature is ready to be born, we feel an energetic pressure for it to happen. We can choose to tend the new life, or we can ignore it and let it die. Mary tended the birth. She

cared for the Christ child. Let us tend the Divine being born in us.

9. Having No Anxiety:
Philippians 4:4–7

The Christmas story is filled with examples of the close presence of the Divine. We can only imagine the anxiety Mary and Joseph, the Wise Men, and the shepherds must have felt as they received the birth of the Christ. They followed the promptings of Divine Messengers and had the protection and shelter needed to honor the new. We are guided every day through the intelligences in our body and mind. We must remember the Divine is near.

10. Being Made New:
Ephesians 4:17–32

Christmas offers an opportunity to seek the birth of the new in our lives. Our call, the call from the Self/God Within, is to be "made new in mind and spirit."

11. One Body:
1 Corinthians 12:27–13:3

The Christmas story is a beautiful reminder of our interconnectedness and how we all matter. Mary and Joseph needed one another to bring the Christ child into the world. The wise men and shepherds were affected; they went to greet and honor the baby Jesus. We affect one another positively as we give birth to the Divine in our nature.

12. Keep Your House In Order:
Isaiah 65:17–25

During the holiday season, we need to be reminded to tend ourselves. We can get separated from ourselves by giving too much. We agree to outer world demands and unrealistic self-expectations. Follow Mary and Joseph's example to tend to what you need.

13. The Union of Opposites:
Psalm 119:89–96

The birth of the Christ brings reconciliation. Within our psyches/souls, something is united every time a bit of the larger Self/God Within is born. We consciously invite the Divine by holding opposing energies in dialogue until the union occurs.

14. The Implanted Word: Knowing from Within:
James 1:17–27

Healing growth begins as we remember the Divine word that is implanted in us. When we recognize that our human personality houses the Divine, we begin to respect all that comes from within us. We trust the flow of our libido (life force); we relate to it as a harbinger of the larger Self/God Within. Mary and Joseph acted on guidance that came only to them. They did not have the affirmation of the outside world. They trusted their experience.

15. Speaking Up:
Job 7:1–21

Job seemed to know that the distress of mind and bitterness of soul he was feeling was not all there was for him. He did not know what to do of his own accord to change it. He called out to God for help. Throughout the Christmas story, we see God's guidance. We can only imagine how many conversations Mary and Joseph must have had with God along the way. We too need to speak up. The Divine Within accompanies us through all.

16. A New Heaven and Earth:
Revelation 21:1–8

The birth of Jesus over 2,000 years ago changed the world. When we allow our selves to give birth to our heart's desires, our worlds are changed. Receiving and trusting the new allows us to know the Divine in our lives.

17. The Divine Is Here:
John 20:1–18

The Self/God Within stands behind, or within, every experience of our body, mind, and psyche/soul. We have only to look with eyes that see the seed of the Divine that has taken shape within us and around us. All who encountered the Christ Child looked with eyes to see the unexpected.

18. Coming into the Light:
1 John 2:1–11

Carl Jung stated, "We do not become conscious by imagining figures of Light. We become conscious by bringing Light to the Darkness." Our willingness to relate to our dark feelings and the unknown stirrings within us is key for transformation. The seasons of Advent and Epiphany occur when we experience the shortest sun-filled days. This is the time we celebrate the birth of the Christ. The birth of the Divine within us occurs at the moments of greatest darkness.

19. Moving Out of the Caves:
1 Kings 19:1–15a

There is a time of retreat when one is giving birth to new life. The new life may show up as a creative project, a love relationship, different interests, or healthier habits. There is also a retreat that is an avoidance of living. Our anxieties about not being all-powerful or in control can trigger withdrawal that stops our growth. We fear encountering the unknown Mystery. The story of Elijah reminds us to stay present to what is; it may be the stirrings of the Divine.

20. Moving into the New:
Acts 18:12–28

In order for new life to emerge, old ways have to move aside. This story from Acts is symbolic of the internal processes of resistance to the new. We see this in the Christmas story where Herod wanted the baby Jesus killed. Mary and Joseph protected the Christ child by taking an alternative route home. We too have to protect the new bits of Self from the **attitudes that seek to destroy it.**

21. Out With the Old and In With the New: Col. 3:1–17

Epiphany means a sudden realization of God has happened. We wake up to the Divine presence in a new way. We cannot make ourselves have an epiphany, but we can cultivate ways of being that facilitate seeing the Divine. The starting point is working with our emotional natures. When we seek the connection to the Self/God Within in whatever we are experiencing, we open to an epiphany.

22. Let the Old Die and the New Grow: Nehemiah 1:1–11

In order for Joseph to wed Mary, he had to let go of his preconceived ideas. Mary's pregnancy before marriage was not the "right" cultural norm. Joseph trusted his encounter with the Divine. He set aside the old beliefs and acted with his heart. We too must let the old go in order to move forward with the new that's life giving.

23. Keeping Covenant:
2 Kings 17:24–41

We think of the birth of the Christ as God's new covenant to his people. Every time a new aspect of our larger Self or

God Within emerges, we are called to live in covenant to the Divine in our nature. Covenant means relationship. Relationship means dialogue. We keep covenant with our Self/God Within by engaging with all aspects of our self.

24. Parable of the Talents: Use What You Have:
Matthew 25:14–30, Luke 19:12–27

In the Christmas story, the innkeeper was creative in finding space for Mary and Joseph. He didn't have a room in the end, so he offered them the stable. It was what he had, and he chose to use it. We can thwart the birth of the Divine in our life by not using what we have. The Parable of the Talents reminds us to risk using what we have even when it doesn't seem enough.

25. Creating Consciousness:
Genesis 32:22–31

The story of Jacob wrestling with the angel is a contrast to the seemingly easy encounter of the angels with Mary and Joseph. There are times in our journey that we are given the blessing of conscious knowing effortlessly. There are other times that we have to want the light of consciousness and fight for it. Our tenacity in holding onto our desire is what brings us the blessing.

26. Following Inner Divine:
Genesis 27:30–45

Mary and Joseph broke with the customs of their day. She was pregnant out of wedlock; Joseph still chose to marry her. Jacob gets something out of order according to the customs of his day. Often, the Self/God Within calls us to step outside the familiar roles that restrict our heart's longings. New life means something changes. The new replaces the old.

27. Oneness of Body and Mind:
2 Corinthians 5:6–10

The spiritual path of the West is Incarnation. The Christmas story celebrates God becoming man. The spiritual and the physical are one and the same; they are just different densities of the same energy. We encounter the Divine first in our embodied experiences. We have to learn to stay consciously aware of our body experience to know the Divine in the world.

28. Living the Truth of Who You Are:
Deuteronomy 3:1–11

When the Christ child was born, old allegiances had to be broken. The wise men did not return to Herod as instructed. Mary and Joseph went home differently than planned. We have to willingly destroy the ways of being and doing that stop us from living the truth of our true Self.

ABOUT THE AUTHOR
KATHLEEN WILEY

Kathleen Wiley is a Jungian Psychoanalyst in private practice in Davidson, North Carolina. She works with individuals, couples, and groups with an eye towards wholeness. Her work seeks to empower people to live out of a conscious connection to God Within as experienced in our body and mind. She is a Senior Training Analyst with the Memphis-Atlanta Jungian Seminar. She is also on the faculty of The Haden Institute. Kathleen's work reflects her journey from being a Director of Christian Education to a Mental Health Counselor to a Jungian Analyst. She has a passion for understanding the Judeo-Christian scriptures as symbolic of movements within our psyche/soul. She writes mediations on the scriptures from this perspective.

Her series NEW LIFE is available through Amazon. Her writings are also accessible at InnerDivineSpirit.com.

About the Cover Photo

Kathleen took the cover photo on her honeymoon, inspired by the opening created by the greenery as she walked towards the beach on Seabrook Island. As she was taking pictures, she saw something zoom across the walkway and later saw a beautiful bird in her photo.

Our encounters with the Inner Divine Spirit sometimes happen like this. They come out of nowhere when our focus is on something else, and we do not know what we experienced until later. The photo seemed like the perfect opening for NEW LIFE.

About Bird Symbology

In Christian symbolism, birds are the souls of humans who have reached a high state of perfection and represent the process of opening up to knowledge and a higher wisdom. Also representative of the future as well as eternal life, birds are considered to be signs of renewal.

Specifically, the oriole (the bird captured in the above-mentioned cover photo) symbolizes the positive attributes of happiness, peace and tranquility. The Blue Jay represents intelligence, determination, and assertiveness. The blue bird is indicative of springtime renewal, cheerfulness, home, hearth and good health. With grace and nobility, the cardinal asks us to stand a little taller and step into our natural confidence as if we were born to lead. The wren, being an active little bird, speaks of energy and vibrancy. Being social, the wren is indicative of enriching life through relationships and making progress each day towards keeping a happy heart whereas the blackbird warns of temptation. Finches, like the wren, also represent high energy. As song birds, finches herald bright days on the horizon. When they sing lightly to the heart, they guide us towards our creative potential and invite us to make our gifts more audible and available to others.